Toni Friedrich

Geoffrey Chaucer's "The Reeve's Tale" - Summary and Linguistic Examination

GRIN Verlag

Bibliografische Information der Deutschen Nationalbibliothek:

Die Deutsche Bibliothek verzeichnet diese Publikation in der Deutschen National-
bibliografie; detaillierte bibliografische Daten sind im Internet über http://dnb.d-
nb.de/ abrufbar.

Imprint:

Copyright © 2007 GRIN Verlag GmbH
Druck und Bindung: Books on Demand GmbH, Norderstedt Germany
ISBN: 978-3-656-09398-5

This book at GRIN:

http://www.grin.com/en/e-book/184586/geoffrey-chaucer-s-the-reeve-s-tale-sum-
mary-and-linguistic-examination

The Reeve´s Tale

1. Who ist the Reeve?

According to the general prologue the Reeve was choleric, i.e. dominated by the humor called choler (or yellow bile), and thus hot-tempered by nature. (Lines 587- 622) → *"The Reve was a sclendre colerik man."* (587)

The Reeve in the prologue: A Reeve was a manager and accountant on an estate or manor and chosen from among the serfs.

As we stated once, several surnames derived from former professions. → Christopher Reeve

Precise description of the Reeve in the general prologue, translated into Modern English: *"Choleric, had a shaved beard, hairs cut off above his ears, his top was cut short like that of a priest, long and thin legs like a staff, no calf was seen. Well could he keep a granary, well he knew by drought and rain the yielding of his seed and his grain, his lords sheep, his cattle, his cows, his pigs, his horses, his livestock and his poultry was wholly under this reeves governing, and by his contract he gave the reckoning since his lord was twenty year of age. No man could bring him in arrears. There was no overseer, nor herdsman, nor other servant that did not know his cunning, and his deceit. They were afraid of him as of the death. His dwelling was fair upon the heath. He knew better than his lord how to increase his possession. He was very rich, he lend his own lord from his own resources in sly ways, he was good in trade and a good craftsman, the reeve sat on a horse that was dappled grey and named Scot. He was from Norfolk and wore a blue coat."* (Lines 587- 622)

The character of the Reeve is also reflected in the prologue of the Reeve's predecessor. The Miller is about to tell his story and the Reeve gets immediately irritated, he says: *"The Reve answerde and seyde, "Stint thy clappe! Lat be thy lewed dronken harloytrye. It is a sinne and eek a greet folye To apeiren any man, or him diffame, And eek to bringen wyves in swich fame. Thou mayst y-noght of othere thinges seyn."* (Lines 36- 41)

1

The Reeve warns the miller not to disparage any man or even to talk lewdly about a woman. His threat indeed is a hypocrisy since the Reeve himself recourses to a disparaging vocabulary in his forthcoming tale.

Chaucer apologizes for the Miller and the Reeve in the Miller's Prologue: *"The Millere is a cherl, ye knowe wel this; So was the Reve eek and othere mo, And harlotrye they tolden bothe two. Avyseth yow and putte me out of blame; And eek men shal nat maken ernest of game."* (74- 78)

Modern English: *"The miller was a churl you well know this; So was the reeve, and many another more, And ribaldry they told from plenteous store. Be then advised, and hold me free from blame; Men should not be too serious at a game."*

2. Summary of the Reeve's Prologue

Chaucer writes that everybody had enjoyed the story of the Miller, which told about a carpenter that is tricked, but with one exception- the Reeve, as he is a carpenter himself: *"Ne at this tale I saugh no man him greve, But it were only Osewold the Reve. By because he was of carpenteres craft, A litel ire in his herte y-laft."* (5- 8)

The Reeve says he could well tell a story in return in which a proud miller is deceived, but he is too old to recourse to such ribaldries: *"If that me liste speke of ribaudye. But ik am old; me list not pley for age."* (12-13)

The Reeve then speaks about his age, for instance: *"Myn herte is also mowled as myne heres"* (16); ME= *"my heart is as mouldy as is my hair"*. And only four embers would still remain: Boasting, lying, anger and avarice. → The Reeve is at least honest about his negative streaks.

He compares his life with a wine cask which tap had started to run a long time ago: *"And ever sithe hath so the tappe y-ronne, Til that almost al empty is the tonne."* (39- 40)

And since he is that old he will not speak with a *"silly tongue"* of wretchedness.

The host replies to the sermon of the Reeve: *"What shul we speke alday of Holy Writ?"* (48)
ME= *"Why must we speak the whole day of holy things?"*
The host is teasing the Reeve again and emphasizes again that the Reeve should at last start
with his tale: *"The devel made a reve for to preche."* (49)

The Reeve says he will pay back force with force. Means he will pay back the insult he had
received beforehand from the Miller: *"Right in his cherles termes wol I speke. I pray to God
his nekke mote tobreke."* (63- 64) → It depicts that the Reeve is indeed choleric and still
irritated.

3. Summary of the tale
At last the tale starts. The Reeve talks about a miller called Simkin, who was *"as eny pecok
he was proud and gay"* (72) and a great swaggerer at markets. The miller protected himself
with a l lot of cutlasses. He was a thief of the grain and meal that people entrusted him to
grind. He was married to the daughter of the parson of the town. She was *"proud, and pert as
is a pye"* (96). And nobody dared to address her because they feared the daggers of the miller.
They had a daughter of 20 years and a six month old son. Chaucer describes the daughter as
"with buttokes brode and brestes rounde" (121). The parson wanted her to be married *"into
som worthy blood of auncetrye".* (128)

The miller had the monopoly of the land as regards malt and wheat. And there was a big
college named Soler Halle that let its wheat and malt ground by the miller. When one time the
manciple was ill, the miller seized the opportunity and stole even more flour and corn. The
warden of the college accused him but the miller said he was innocent.

Then there were two students (John and Alain) of the college who were hardy and bold and
asked the warden for leave. They said they wanted to observe the miller and prevent that he
steal anything. The warden complies.

The two blokes went to the miller and said him that they wanted him to grind their corn, as
they expect that the manciple will die soon. They state that they will stand right beside the
funnel to look how the corn runs in (out of interest as they feign). The miller says: *"But, by
my thrift, yet shall I blere hire ye"* (195)

The miller goes out and unties the bridle of the boys´ horse, which immediately dashes off. The boys are in a fuss and forget all their flour. John is blaming Alain and the both of them run behind the horse in order to catch it.

The miller, happy due to the success of his design, orders his wife to knead bread of the flour: *"Yet can a millere make a clerkes berd"* (242)

The boys at last manage to get their horse in the dusk of the day. John knows that they had been beguiled and he fears that they will call them fools. Into the bargain the boys know that they have to beg the miller for lodging and food, ready to spend silver for it.

All of them sup and drink till they are drunk and all of them go to bed at last and the miller, his wife and his daughter fall asleep immediately. As they all lay in their beds, Alain says to John that he will seek some redress for all the mischief that had been done to them. He intends to rape the daughter lying beside them. While Alain is having his fun, John is mourning that he is too scared to join his friend.

The wife of the miller then had to go out to go to the rest room. When she returns she mistakes the beds and settles down in the bed of the clerks. John places himself besides her and they have sexual intercourse. → lewd depiction of Chaucer: *"So mery a fit ne hadde she nat ful yore; he priketh harde and depe as he were mad."* (381- 82)

Alain awakes and says good bye to Melanie, the daughter. Melanie discloses him that they made bread of their own flour and tells him where he can find it.

Alain rises and intends to go back to his friend John not to betray himself. But as he beholds the bed wherein John and the miller's wife lay together, he mistakes John as the Miller and thought he went lost during the night. Thus, he goes right into the bed of the miller, because he lies alone and says to the miller: *"Thou, John, thou swynes-heed, awak for Christes saule, and heer a noble game. For by that lord that called is Seint Jame, As I have thryes in this shorte night Swyved the milleres doghter bolt upright, Whyl thow hast as a coward been agast."* (413- 418)

4

When the miller hears that he jumps up and grasps the throat of Alain. They fight until the miller trips on a stone and falls right on his wife. The wife mistakes the miller with one of the clerks and gives him a blow. The boys flee and take their flour with them. The miller is therefore punished at length for his deceiving behaviour and the reeve closes his tale with the proverb: *"Him thar nat wene wel that yvel dooth; A gylour shal himself bigyled be."* (471- 72) ME= *"He need not expect good who does evil."*

4. Sources

That kind of story is called a *cradle-trick* story and was very popular throughout the late MA and the Renaissance. Some stories have survived, although mostly anonym.

4.1 The Miller and the Two Clerics

There were two poor fellows and friends and deacons of a woodland church. Once they had hard times to suffer, they had no possession and didn't know where to go. The two friends decide that they get a bushel of wheat and a mare on credit from friends to make bread of it. But when they approach the mill the miller hides and his wife tells the clerics that they had to search for him in the nearby woods. During the search the miller steals the mare and the wheat and hides both in his barn. The clerics finally came back and find their property stolen, but they don't suspect the miller. The miller, touched by some reproaches, offers them the floor to sleep in. The miller had a wonderful daughter who he used to lock up in his cupboard to protect her from the outer world. He always passes the key through an aperture to her afterwards and then goes asleep. As in the tale of Chaucer, all of them go to bed after they had supper. But one of the clerks, who had watched the fair daughter locked up, goes to her a couple of minutes later.

He scratches her door and tells her that he had got a ring (indeed, the ring from the andiron) which retains virginity for that one who wears it. In order to get it she opens the door and both of them had their pleasure during the night. A little later the miller's wife arises and passes by the other cleric who decides to seek the same pleasure as his friend. So he carries the baby, who the miller and his wife had, to his bedroom and when the wife goes back to her bed he squeezes the baby's ear in order to make it cry. The wife confoundedly goes into the direction of the baby's cry and places herself in the bed beside the baby where the cleric was waiting for her (= sexual intercourse). The end is again quite similar to that of the Reeves tale. The clerk, who returns from the cupboard, mistakes the miller's bed at his own and insinuates the miller what he had done. Enraged the miller fights with him but the cleric was the stronger one. At the end, the wife discloses that the miller had stolen everything from the clerics, whereupon they beat him up severely, catch their possessions and go to another mill to let the wheat be grinded.

4.2 Giovanni Boccaccio - From the Decameron; The Story of Pinuccio and Adriano

Pinuccio was in love with a girl of a wealthy man and she also loved him. But Pinuccio was afraid that he could disgrace the girl so he makes up a design. He takes a friend of him and goes to the house of the father of his love in order to spend a night there to get acquainted to the layout of the house in order to be able to sneak in whenever it pleases him. The host lodges his guests in a very narrow old bed. But as soon as Pinuccio considers the host to be asleep, he sneaks into the bed of his love. Adriano, obliged by a physical need, arises a little later and in order to get through a passage he displaces a cradle which indicated the bed of the host. Similar to the other stories, the wife mistakes the beds and Adriano seized that opportunity to have pleasure with her and she welcomes him.

And again, Pinuccio, lays himself beside the host and tells him that he had pleased his love six times. The host awakes and quarrels with him. The wife recognizes her mistake, sneaks into the bed of the daughter and pretends to have just been dragged out of sleep. She screams to her husband that she had slept all the night beside the daughter and Pinuccio must therefore be a liar. Adriano, getting the plan, yelled at his friend to stop wandering and telling of his dreams at night. Pinuccio, also getting the plan, now pretends to somnambulate. At the end the hosts believes all of them and everything is fine again.

5. Linguistic Aspects of the Reeve's Tale

Within the rather short story of the Reeve there are a lot of examples which depict many particularities of Middle English. Some of those examples are listed below.

5.1 Etymological Origins of Some Terms

Laughen: 1 *"When folk had laughen at this nyce cas"* → O.E. *hlæhhan*

Carpenter: 7 *"By cause he was of carpenteres craft"* → O.N.Fr. *carpentier*, L.L. *carpentarius* "wagon maker," from L. *carpentum* "two-wheeled carriage, cart," maybe today related to ME "car"

Blame:	9 *"He gan to grucche and blamed it a lyte"* → O.Fr. *blasmer* "to speak evil of", L.L. *blasphemare* "revile, reproach"
Fruit:	18 *"The ilke fruit is ever lenger the wers"* → O.Fr. *fruit*, from L. *fructus* "fruit, produce, profit,"
Anger:	30 *"Avaunting, lying, anger, coveityse."* → O.N. *angra* "to grieve, vex;"
Host:	45 *"Whan that oure Host hadde herd this sermoning"* → O.Fr. *hoste* "guest, host", L. *hospitem* (nom. *hospes*) "guest, host,"
Tale:	51 *"Sey forth thy tale, and tarie nat the tyme"* → O.E. *talu* "story, tale, the action of telling,"
Peril:	78 *"Ther was no man for peril dorste him touche"* → O.Fr. *peril*, L. *periculum* "an attempt, risk, danger,"
Face:	80 *"Round was his face, and camus was his nose"* → O.Fr. *face*, V.L. **facia*, from L. *facies* "appearance, form, figure"
Marriage:	126 *"And straunge he made it of hir marriage"* → O.Fr. *mariage*, V.L. **maritaticum*, from L. *maritatus*, pp. of *maritatre* "to wed, marry, give in marriage"
Disport:	189 *"Into the trough; that sal be my disport"* → Anglo-Fr. *disporter* "divert, amuse," from O.Fr. *desporter*, lit. "carry away" (the mind from serious matters), from *des-* "away" + *porter* "to carry", L. *portare* "to carry"
Felawes:	258 *"Bathe the wardeyn and our felawes alle"* → O.E. *feolaga* "partner", O.N. *felagi*, from *fe* "money" + verbal base denoting "lay". Sense is of "one who puts down money with another in a joint venture."
Place:	271 *"Lat see now if this place may suffyse"* → O.E. "open space in a city, market place, square," from O.Fr. *place*, from M.L. *placea* "place, spot," from L. *platea* "courtyard, open space, broad street,"

7

Chambre:	285 *"And in his owene chambre hem made a bed"* → O.Fr. *chambre*, from L.L. *camera* "a chamber, room" → camera in Mod. L. *camera obscura* "dark chamber"
Cradle:	307 *"The cradle at his beddes feet is set"* → O.E. *cradol* "little bed"
Pisse:	366 *"And gan awake, and wente hir out to pisse"* → O.Fr. *pissier* "urinate"
Disparage:	422 *"Who dorste be so bold to disparage"* → O.Fr. *desparagier* "reduce in rank, degrade,"
Fight:	442 *"Help, Simkin, for the false clerkes fighte"* → O.E. feohtan "to fight" → today German: "fechten"
Proverb:	470 *"And therefore this proverb is seyd ful sooth"* → O.Fr. *proverbe*, from L. *proverbium* "a common saying," lit. "words put forward," from *pro-* "forth" + *verbum* "word"
Majesty:	473 ,,*And god, that sitteth heighe in magestee"* → O.Fr. *majeste* "grandeur, nobility," from L. *majestatem* (nom. *majestas*) "greatness, dignity, honor, excellence," from stem of major (neut. *majus*), comp. of *magnus* "great."

5.2 Pronunciation

- 199 *"In stide of flour, yet wol I yeve hem bren."* → <ou> pronounced [u:]; French influence

- 1 *"Whan folk had laughen at this nyce cas"*
  204 *"Whan that he saughte his tyme, softely"*

    → <gh> pronounced [x], here <h> as a diacritical sign after French and Latin pattern (sign without no sound, but indicating a special sound) e.g. <th>

- 206 *"The clerkes hors, ther it stood y-bounde"* → <oo> pronounced [o:]; also evidence French influence

- 201 *"The gretteste clerkes been noght wysest men"* → <ee> pronounced [e:]

- 79 *"A Sheffeld thwitel baar he in his hose"* → <aa> pronounced [a:]

- 309 *"And whan that dronken al was in the crouke"* → <o> in vicinity of <n, m, v, w> is pronounced [u] just like in <sonne> → derived from Caroline minuscule (to much vertical lines)

- 16 *"Myn herte is also mowled as myne heres"* → <w> after vowels pronounced as [u]

- 42 *"The sely tonge may wel ringe and chimbe"* → <ng> pronounced [n] + [g] if medial sound as in this case

5.3 Morphology

- 1 *"Whan folk had laughen at this nyce cas"* → Pl. past participle, without past participle indicating y-

- 4 *"But, for the more part, they loughe and pleyde"* → sound change indicating past and -d(e) past suffix; other past indicating suffixes → -ed(e), -t(e)

- 5 *"Ne at this tale I saugh no man him greve"* → again sound change within

- 7 *"By cause he was of carpenteres craft"* → -es ending → genitive

- 11 *"With blering of a proud milleres ye"* → genitive again

- 8 *"A litel ire is in his herte y-laft"* → y indicates past participle

- 16 *"Myn herte is also mowled as myne heres"* → Plural –es, –is and –en as in eyen

- 28 *"Yet in oure asshen olde is fyr y-reke"* → Plural ending –en

- 14 *"Gras-tyme is doon, my fodder is now for**age**"* → French suffix

- 421 *"Thou shalt be deed, Goddes digni**tee**"* → French suffix

- 143 *"For ther-biforn he stal but curteis**ly**"* → -ly for adverbs

- 97 *"And, only for **hire** mirthe and revelrye"*
  462 *"And at the mille yet they toke **hir** cake"*
  158 "And at the laste the wardeyn yaf **hem** leve"

  → Chaucer uses the nominative *"thei"* but retains the native forms for possessive and accusative "*hir(e)*" or *"her(e)"* instead of *"their"*, *"hem"* instead of *"them"*. The <h> is only weakly pronounced.

- 171 *"And John also, how now, what do **ye** heer?"*
  392 *"But er **thou** go, o thing I wol **thee** telle."*
  418 *"Whyl **thow** hast as a coward been agast."*

  → Second-person pronouns have both singular forms *"thou"* (also *"thow"*), *"thy"* or *"thyn"*, *"the(e)"* – and plural forms *"ye"*, *"youre"*, or *"yow"*. The letter set can be used with singular meaning in some case.

- 285 *"And in his owene cham**br**e hem made a bed"* → later matethesis

- 470 *"And therefore this proverbe is seyd ful **sooth"*** → today only a fixed compound constituent "soothsayer"

- 70 *"And this is verray **soth** that I yow telle."* → heterogenous spelling, maybe due to metre

- 85 *"A theef he was for sooth**e** for corn and mele."* → remnant of O.E. masculine dative ending

10

- On page 43 of *A Book of Middle English* by Burrow and Turville-Petre, it is state that the suffix *"-self"* does not refer to a reflexive pronoun, but to reinforce the pronoun. In The Reeve's Tale *"-self"* is used like in ME.

→ 173 *"Him boes (behooves) serve him**selve** that has no sway (servant)"*
    472 *"A gylour (beguiler) shal him**self** bigyled be"*

5.4 Syntax

Though S-V-O order is mostly used, Chaucer's ME word order is very arbitrary which helps to build fitting metre.

Subject Complement – Subject – Verb: 85 *"A theef he was for sothe..."*

Object – Verb – Subject: 79 *"A Sheffeld thwitel baar he in his hose."*

Modal Verb – Subject – Verb- Object: 242 *"Yet can a millere make a clerkes berd..."*

Adverb – Subject – Verb: 399 *"... almost she gan to wepe."*

Complement – Object – Subject – Verb: 447 *"And by the wal a staf she fond anon..."*

Complement – Subject – Verb – Object: 462 *"And at the mille yet they toke hir cake"*

Verb – Subject – Subject Complement: 464 *"Thus is the proude millere wel y-bete,"*

References:
- Burrow, John A. / Thorlac, Turville- Petre. *A Book of Middle English*. Oxford: Blackwell.
- Kolve, V. A. and Glenden Olson eds. *The Canterbury Tales: A Norton Critical Edition*. New York and London: Norton.
- Markus, Manfred. *Mittelenglisches Studienbuch*. Tübingen: Francke.
- http://www.etymonline.com